MAKING BONES WALK

poems

Alex Boyd

Luna Publications

Library and Archives Canada Cataloguing in Publication

Boyd, Alex
Making Bones Walk / Alex Boyd. 1st ed
Poems.

ISBN 13: 978-0-9781471-1-2
ISBN 10: 0-9781471-1-1

I. Title.

A CIP catalogue record for this book is available
from Library and Archives Canada.

Design and typesetting by Sean Tai
Cover design by Sean Tai
Front cover art by Aleksander Bukvic

Printed and bound in Canada
This book is printed on acid free paper.

Luna Publications
43 Gifford St.
Toronto, ON
M5A 3H9
www.lunapublications.com

Distributed by spdbooks.org

To my father, James Boyd

CONTENTS

ACKNOWLEDGEMENTS

Thank you to Goran Simic for starting Luna Publications and publishing this book, it has meant a great deal to have a writer I respect so deeply offer to put it out in the world. Thank you to Fraser Sutherland for the careful, perceptive and diplomatic editing of the poems in this book. And many thanks to Aleksander Bukvic, Mariela Griffor, Sean Tai and everyone involved in producing this book.

Thank you to the Ontario Arts Council for the financial support.

Thanks to the editors of various magazines who published earlier versions of some of these poems: *Ink Magazine*, *WORD*, *Jones Av*, *The Annex Echo*, *Taddle Creek*, *The Antigonish Review*, *Nthposition.com*.

Thank you to Wayson Choy for all your kindness and support, and for being such a stellar teacher radio broadcasting no longer seemed like the way to go. To Paul Vermeersch for being supportive, and for trusting me with the IV lounge reading series, which has been a pleasure. Thank you to Dani Couture for being a great friend but also for routinely providing valuable, diplomatic advice on poems. To Myna Wallin and David Clink for the encouragement and support through publishing some of these poems in a chapbook called *Brick and Bone*, it was an honour. Thank you to Carmine Starnino for being supportive and for perceptive advice on the poems. In the literary community I've also deeply appreciated the friendship and support of Shaun Smith, Michael Bryson, Matthew Tierney, Todd Swift.

I couldn't have asked for a better family of kind and generous people and I thank them all. "Lines" is dedicated to my father James Boyd, with thanks for the example of a good man. Thank you to my continually supportive friends who are as important to me as family, you know who you are, and you mean the world to me.

And thank you for reading this. Keep making your bones walk.

MAKING BONES WALK

EACH DAY THE SMALL GODS

Each day the small gods all come forward,
float small rafts of ideas, loaded
with words, some rolling overboard.
Two small gods meet and make
a third – my father inhales to speak
on my voicemail and I remember
he gave me breath. Small gods know
nothing will stop tomorrow from sliding in,
the night rolls fiercely around outside
and they aren't foolish enough to believe
it thinks of them. Small gods stop
to see something important in the eyes
of a tiny, trembling dog, overhear words.
They sense talk falling all around you,
collecting on your eyebrows, so that you,
small god, have to shake it off like a dog.
Small gods lose memories, find them again,
like broken benches under melting snow.
Wonder about, claim to know larger gods,
who must have had an unknown reason
to slide wind onto a mist of rain, fill air
with drops screaming happily in decay.
Small gods are clean as bursting through paper.
A circus dwarf on a strong man's shoulders
belongs to small gods who know the strength
of the elbow, work from there. They reach out
with small arms, a few feet in every direction.

FINE PRINT FOR THE BACK OF A BIRTH CERTIFICATE

A man throws his weight against the world, as if
at the bow of a great ship – and everyone changes
the course of history or no one at all.

Money will determine everything you do, or don't –
there will be days you will protect a coin
in your pocket as though it's the last nail.

Kiss in front of a bust in a park, and you're married –
a photo, if taken as proof, must capture the scarf
of trees, the five worry lines on the helpless head.

(High collar and four brown donut buttons are optional
if a silent fire engine pulls itself across the earth
the way a drop of blood would roll down an arm).

You should find a way to make it illegal for a lawyer
to brush past an old lady on the street, and for any
one person to have more than a million dollars.

Don't think old men with grey hair are wise –
some place a small ribcage for flowers near the window.
And pain is free but try not to be afraid.

LESSON

When I arrived my friends had already given
each of them names: *Edgar* or some such thing.
You had to look for the strands the tiny green worms
dropped down on – nearly invisible – thin as wishes.
Each boy with a sliver of life that crawled on a finger.

The weaker boy – trusting – loaned me his, and I watched
the tiny thing twist like a living musical note
before I crushed it, finding (aside from the gasp
I knew the weak boy would make) that it was really
nothing at all between my fingers, not
the slightest pressure, a small green stain – how easily

life snaps shut, as quick as closing a book.
And how my power was gone as soon as I used it.

SPRINGS OF INSTINCT

It's a world with dead cats, no point trying
to deny it, a world that creates these soft
dangerous springs of instinct and then
lets them decay, without them knowing
anything about it, maybe a puzzling moment
when it can't manage the same kind of leap.
I killed one. It was suddenly in front of my car,
a flash of orange paint on the air, a thump.
My friend lost hers for days, it returned
with a mangled leg that had to be removed,
but it simply sat thinking under a chair
for a long time, then became the same princess
it was before, crying out orders, jerking
across rooms faster than you'd expect.
I loved its old fragment of Pharaoh soul.

Going to sleep each night, I want that key,
the secret to new rooms of understanding,
rather than staring through flat oyster keyholes
with thick coats of yearly deepened paint.
But something inside me trips me up, I dream
instead of arguments, of accidents, stepping
out of a car to look at a dead cat, its tongue
sticking out at me forever, body giving
one final twitch and my own appalled cry.
I want to tell my friend her now-dead cat is there,
behind the air, gone to a world where mice
can't fire their drunken bodies into hiding.
I want to say that but all I know for sure
is it's a world with dead cats, a world
that gives things, and takes them away.

DARKER IN THIS ROOM

Lying here it is darker in this room
than the night outside as blue as the sea
and forced into a square shape by my window,
arm's shadow a snake kicked at the elbow
and the wet prattle and tap of the rain
sounding just like the snapping of a fire
(which I had never noticed)

(and the thought of death arrives as the cool air
of a breeze slips in from the world outside)

noticing the moon outside left behind
like a bright fingerprint and wondering
when you die, do all the threads of thinking
unfinished, untucked, bumping to the ground
push up to an answer, hit your forehead
or is it something else, something silent
(thicker darkness than this room)

MAN IN A BLACK COAT

No longer just a home for seals or stage for birds,
the sea wakes up, lifts white hands and shatters
its own stretching fingers against the stone
harbour walls that circle little fishing boats.
Sailors had special words for certain things
to step carefully around bad luck – you didn't say
minister, you said man in a black coat.
Ninety years ago, here in Arbroath, Scotland,
my Nana was born – and in the twenty-six years
I'd know here I would never ask her about it.

Three hundred years ago, the sea beat the harbour,
carried great horns of wind that tore it apart.
It was just yesterday to the sea, the last time
it noticed this pretty little town, and at the same
time, remembered every wave is a muscle.
Now I stand in my own beginning, the spot on the map
where the line begins, and maybe for the first time
this place sees me too, the air forced around me.
If only I could know how it judges me,
not so much the town, that one great body – the sea.

SHAPES OF AIR

Air takes the shape of a house's interior,
the edges of candlesticks, and outside it moves
in (moves away) in all directions,
making note of the shape of outside.
It does this for all things. Opening
a window, we miss watching square pillows
of air enter the room, or the air instantly
wanting to know the spaces my arm leaves
as I move to turn on a light switch.
The air memorizes us, sits on the edge

of each second. Passing two people
on the street, it allows the fragment
of conversation I overhear, the words carried
by an invisible crowd to my ear.
If I demand of the air that my head turns
back to look at a woman, the air holds my chin,
turns it like a lover. Air goes into me,
lets me move as I will despite holding two
fingers deep in my lungs. It holds me up
like a puppet, yet follows me like a dog.

HEAT AND LIGHT

Sunlight steps down, greets every part of us,
so we ignore it. If it was just a little harder
someone would make us buy bars of it,
unwrap one each morning over coffee.
Dinosaurs lost the sun – an asteroid
arrived before there were words or coins, threw
so much earth into sky that instead of sun
the ice age came. One of the things
I know from my short time in this place
is that one city block makes the difference
between homes the size of asteroids
and people begging on bright winter streets.
I gave change to a man who shifted from one
foot to another, he didn't say thanks
for the change but said thanks for not ignoring me.
I said no problem, walked away knowing
I'd done next to nothing. Stepping outside
on days like this, I thank the good little pain
as sunlight kicks in the doors of my eyes.

SHINE

Notice. Bring anyone to know a spring night
where the rain stepped down over everything
and the air remembers. Down there, trees curve
into a kind of sky, and below, streetlights
(low stars we made) help the street shine.

The world is beautiful when it moves quietly,
as though asleep. Remember a field, you walked
into pockets of life, the birds that would launch
out of tall grass, move together in flight, fold
and open again. Remember being in tangled sheets,
pinching her flesh at the bottom of the tattoo to see
if it actually looks like you hold a rose (if you did,
you'd give it to her). A cooler season runs
across your back each time she exhales, while
you fight the urge to sigh angrily, let your feelings
whistle through you, use you like a kettle.

Remember when for no reason you leaned forward
to kiss her body and then sat back to notice
the small trace of your saliva catching the light.
And, in remembering, you notice it again.
Look. Where you kissed her. It shines.

GREAT BLACK DOGS

Held down by the horizon, poised
and staring off the edge of a bluff
I remember it – I stared also,
out the back car window, the ground
rising, swelled over him –
that black dog, near our cottage home,
summers in New Brunswick when
I was young, visiting my grandparents.
Cut open, the memory lets out the hiss
of a casual wind through trees,
my brother and I defending the beach.

But he's dead, my mother says later
after all those summers have been stacked
like plates. We are in the house
to move my grandmother to an old age
home, picking through rusted things
in my grandfather's garage –
he's been dead for years, she adds.

Months after my mother died I woke
to her voice calling my name. One word
balanced on the edge of a dream, a cork
on a wave. I remember her laugh, struck
easily as a wooden match, the strongest
details coming back first like the tallest parts
of a ship, unsinking. Things I go back for
like bread. *Can you pull hard enough
to bring someone back?* That black dog

was old, then. It knew, eyes sweeping over
the roll of things like a soft cloth.

And that black dog is still there.

BRIDE OF FRANKENSTEIN

These discs are the best use for technology,
forget sending businessmen to England
in four hours, they'll just want to go in three.
Here's how it works: the disc spins,
and for every little Boris there's a little Bride
deep in the silver, somewhere under
your reflection, the worry lines on your brow.
They meet and spin and the film starts to play.
So what if Lon Chaney is a plump Wolf Man,
or the body count just isn't all that high.
In the days before quantity meant more,
murdering a few people made you evil.
And so what if the Lugosi Dracula is staked
off camera, heads turning – you don't need
to see every bloody thing, now do you.
Again the villagers are back with torches,
tearing down signs all over town,
Assistant needed: must be hunchbacked,
have two years experience pulling levers.
Boris doesn't scare me – I'm taking him
to stand there, right at the entrance
where the world pours thickly into my dreams,
his instructions: smash all the unhappiness.

THE CURVE OF EAR

Enough strange courage
to hold herself against the wind,
the rest of us passing bent and unnoticed
by the woman dressed in black
standing out like a lever, pausing
to speak sideways into air to her dead husband
while pulling the groceries home.

At lunch, lying in a first sun of the year
that paints the inside of my closed eyelids
orange, I am in a pool of sound
and the car starting taps me
when it would not have reached
my thoughts at all, mixes
with broken ladders of talk.

An elevator at work that day stops
for five long minutes,
buries me alone in the silent heart
of a spinning place, with a phone
that hooks me up to voices that can't hear me,
asking can I help you (twice)
before hanging up.

Again underpaid colleagues
try to speak to wealthy employers
about how they have trouble
affording new boots for winter
while the same shuffle of explanation is prepared.

And I remember one night

when my finger traced the carved
bowl of your ear, wanting
to know each heated, bending line
that steps out for my voice.

MAKING BONES WALK

Tonight I was surprised by my skull,
was brushing my hair and noticed it there,
thin and blind to what can come crashing –
waiting for the nest of a pillow
to have all the movement drop away.

Poor bones are pulled along in the dark,
don't know when they cross at a streetlight,
cars waiting behind invisible gates,
that fragile belief in decency, thrown out
twice a day at rush hour, headlights
glaring, cotton-tails of fumes beating ground
while sets of hooked up bones start walking.

Bones know they jumped but don't hear
the cry of the car, see the passing iron.
In an old dream I was nestled under tar
with only a straw to breathe – and I knew
that dream belonged to my bones.

POSSIBILITIES

It's possible we could be scientists in love,
dopamine elbowing into my frontal cortex,
chemical messengers bringing envelopes
and papercuts, living red dashes of hush
and breathing: love is when you know
your name is safe in someone else's mouth.
Both love and madness slide with serotonin,
adrenalin, the letters in *slave* milling through
larger, groping words, *saliva.*
The hunched shoulders of my building wanting
to push everyone but you away. And
I could be on a leaning train, thinking.
The strangers like sparrows all around.
A train that groans and pulls like a mule,
knows tunnels of midnight get to brightness,
the moment I kissed your soft lips and wanted
nothing else, at least for that moment.
You make me want this world, each test
tube and tree above a battered, toxic van.
My holy oxytocin, my lovely vassopressin.

THE BAKER SIGNED UP, 1914

When he stumbles in the trench
his hands cut into mud like dough.
Surrounded by puddles, rats, lice.

Helping carry wounded along wooden
planks because the mud is deep
enough to swallow a man,
he pictures it baked in the sun, hard.

He skips, sometimes, around shell
casings, oven hot and tumbling
from the back of a spent gun.

Under the familiar whistle of
falling bombs that softened
and pounded earth, he slept
while explosions sliced at the edges
of his dreams: the song of chimes
above the door, the smell of fresh bread,
a Chelsea bun with icing dropped
into a paper bag and handed
over the counter.

ALIVE ONE EVENING

Inside air sweet and harder with smoke,
we circle plain tables, balance coffee
into a free spot. You say something
I partly catch, then slowly run thumb
and fingers down your cheeks (like I do
when thinking, as if I had a beard)
and I wonder if you felt that soft brush
of your own thoughts, but I'm sure
your mind was caught on something else.
The room is painted with a constant stream
of mixed words, each fading from the surface
like a sinking stone, dreams after
the alarm of morning. We step outside
and into a breeze, ice-cream-truck happy,
splitting to cover us both, streaming past
and moving on – but before it flutters out
we soak it up, let it smooth us over.

WHAT I KNOW ABOUT GOD

I know that my love had to memorize
our father comma who art in
heaven semicolon. I remember
saying *take care* to the back
of a man, mostly a stranger who
I will never see again. When
she threw back her head I imagined
a voice saying *oh, let the old*
woman have a laugh. Leaving
three vials of blood with the doctor,
felt like giving them three
of my secrets. I know in a small
cemetery in Ireland at dusk while
wind found the trees through low
branches something kept flashing
past the corner of my eye. What
we know is about the size
of the circle that a lantern kicks out
against the night. In Ireland I wrote
one line – *God has a door here.*
But the rest of the words wouldn't come.

OUTSIDE

Outside my window a bus followed a cyclist,
slowly, like a whale behind a swimmer
as if pausing to enjoy the moment it will brush by.
A man, tall and swelling in a ski jacket
points and gives an order to a squirrel.

Walking outside, I see the man feeding pigeons
who is a sun, the centre of the burst,
until they settle in, ignore him over food
and he becomes a background hill.
This was almost a poem called *City*,
given the poster of a thin model in jeans,
EAT spraypainted across her, the ghost
of a sheet of plastic caught in wind.

But many things won't settle into a poem,
glue together – crisp letter shapes grouped
in line and held on the page, or like rainwater
collecting in some rusty bucket and not soaking
back into the earth. There is more, outside.

LINES

I remember learning the King used to be
second only to God and drew a diagram
with lines dropping down to boxes from GOD
to KING, just like that, but the name
of the teacher, what class it was, how old
I'd have been is gone – the memory alone.

I sat with my father to watch TV one night
and cannot remember the program at all,
though as always, I was aware of FATHER
and SON, and when on the show a man stabbed
another, suddenly my father's brow furrowed
in an expression that said *why on earth*

would someone want to do that? and how
sometimes, one action can explain a man
for you despite distance, a quiet wire of talk,
to see that troubled brow, how to grow up
with my father was to know the example
of a good man – and thank God for that.

TRAP DOOR DAYS

dates are just our little picket fences, really

but this one reminds me of an earlier one

from high school when I stood on a streetcorner and waited

next to an old man like this until he turned

sharply and said I hope you don't grow up

and lose your wife like I did that's a terrible

thing and by the way hit those books

well I like school and get pretty good marks I lied

and he said well good but this

old guy looks at me, walks on

nothing much happens until sleep curls around me

that night and I'm reminded with no string

for my balloon I fall through a day

and disappear never remember myself

WALKING DISTANCE

The summer day is starting to stretch
    out like an old cat and
walking north on Grace to Bloor I pass
the man teaching his son to blow bubbles
on the front lawn, the two English girls
with long clean limbs who leap on their dog
when he tries to eat a glass bottle, the man
who sits up on his couch, on the phone
just in time to see me as I pass,

the first one to see me, thanks, and I'm here
and gone again, passing the two girls who
march down the sidewalk as if I don't exist
so that I move aside, almost fall off it

and passing the fat man in the outfield
who raises his glove, somehow knowing it will
    come straight to him,
somehow in step with everything I don't
know, the long slow pull of summer
the whole reason I don't matter.

PUSHING

for William Stafford

This is how it begins: you surface
out of darkness and look around,
the air as close around your head
as two hands with a mood.

Sometimes the mood is dark.
In the night things are moving
and banging that you can't identify.
Anything could open your chest
and place a container there.
Your head turns at the sound
of a dog barking, somewhere.

The next day you find a smooth place
to push a little, remember parts of you
are hidden everywhere, in all the eyes
that catch you, your father watching
you grow, spend time leaning in places
here, or there, how his eyes would tap
on you like an extra heartbeat.

Then at a certain point,
you notice your movements
shifting air, lifting
all the paper edges of the world.

YOU ARE SUMMER

First, the ads demand summer is here.
On streets lit with summer heat, a man
with an ice cream cone attaches himself
to a phone – in his poem we drop into
summer hoping to be young and fail.

Part of her face is missing, covered up
by sunglasses, then red lips step aside
and she blows a strange dark kiss, a pin
of smoke on the world through the open
window as her car spreads across my eye.

That soft wish of smoke pushing to reach
my ears, even a thick summer needs
to fit into the little windows of our senses –
here comes desire, train fast, surrounding
itself, building the invisible tracks it runs on.

Sitting outside on cool nights, or arriving
home to be embraced by damp hands
of sweat reminding me of myself –
underneath, summer is what you do
and it is only convinced of this much.

WORLD IS RIVERS

You wait for something, let it carry you
as though you caught a bus.
Every space a river – step into one and sail,
fall into another and fight.
At first I thought there was one magnet,
fate pulling you to the end of your life.
But you watch people, your friends
change direction, branch away.
You think they tried to wave, arm flashing
between trees, blade of land between you,
aisles of books and sun, dust and cuts.
Rivers that dry up, branches that end.
The last day of university I waited
for my ride, watched cars arrive one
by one like sharks to floating survivors
and take away everyone but me.
Each of us is always the only one left.
And now, needing to quit a place
I sink into, water stumbling to get over
my mouth, in my ears. The shore is a blur
but there must be something there.
A place is a river,
and I have been too long in this one.

NEW WORLD

I noticed my boots were cracked and worn,
that the white haired priest no longer stands
on the front steps of the church I pass
as if watching from the bow of a ship.
The cry of sirens has replaced the cicada.
A city has no great flocks unfolding to cries,
we have the dial tone, the long final moan
of something undefined. No stars,
just one green eye on my computer at night,
a pierced calm, a new undefined world.
The small helicopter of a dragonfly lands
on a crushed cigarette and a boy kicks
a stone until he doesn't feel like kicking it,
and I know somehow, for some reason
you now say a dragonfly looks like a helicopter,
not the other way around. Worst thing
about change, at times you can't remember
what came before. The new world grows over
the old one. A man on the street forced
out a flurry of words that fell together,
snared in his mouth like hares however fast
he pushed them out. *That guy sniffs paint,*
my friend said, and what frightens me most
is that the man still thinks he makes sense.
I'm slowly born into a new world, and watch
for meaning in the way the old one falls.

TWENTY THREE MINUTES FOR EVERYTHING

Weekends I pull off the heavy strings of sleep,
a few at a time, sit without having to suddenly
think *twenty-three minutes for everything:*
Enough time to notice the spider crossing great
blue hills of my shirt unaware it is watched
as its legs hesitate, cycle over uncertainty,
for the second spider broken on the edge of the tub
like a dead sailor on the beach, the third that hangs
quietly in the air as I shower, notes the abrupt
weather, makes geometry with thin legs.
Enough time to remember the end of summer,
and saying goodbye to a friend, a cab to the airport,
the stomach lurching thickness of heat,
our driver hitting the brakes every twenty feet,
somehow continually surprised by the traffic
while jets stitch blue sky like needles above,
split the air with enough noise to prevent thought.
Enough time to think twenty-three minutes
is all missiles would need were they upset,
and coming to complain, for pushing change
off the edge of my desk not quite into my hand
so that dimes hit the ground and dash away
like frightened children, enough time to notice
the red warning flag when I cut myself shaving,
for finding keys, shutting the door, telling myself
my friend will be back soon, even suddenly,
that life will go flying by, and if I am afraid
today, every day falls, for gathering what I can
of my nightmares to scatter at my feet as I walk.

INVENTORY OF A BASEMENT APARTMENT, AFTER BEING EVICTED

Outside the walls, family and friends,
a few good ones, the barbers all over the city
that each know a fragment of my life – the serious
Romanian barber who commented on a child
he didn't move or nothing and I said
he was patient, only to regret what sounded
like a correction – *he was patient,* the barber repeated,
snipped the air and turned back to size up my head.
My old family doctor who retired and disappeared
and the new one, almost my age who smiles
like open arms, the woman who thanked me
at work saying you've been like an angel.

In here, a lineup of Bond films, Connery perfect
in how he pulls off the wetsuit to reveal the tux,
four new walls to protect me, keep warm mice bones
hidden in the ceiling, paperwork I'll never want to see
again, the heating duct that wants to crack my forehead
but can't, the cold painted floors, the electric motor
of coffee in my heart because we're to keep going,
the thought I was buried for the sake of money.
The thin but growing river of bitterness in me,
the desire to hit someone a slightly stronger weed
in my heart each time another homeless tosses me
a nasty remark as I work my way back here.

WE ARE MADE OF LANGUAGE

Adrift, this writing moved through air to find you.
but first I found my way to this writing,
spent days and ended them, knowing
that a bedsheet lifting to cover a body takes air
like a sail, and that for a moment inside you
every atom becomes a letter the instant you say anything,
turn to the word sleep and chains of
those five letters fool together in your body,
while outside us each wish climbs whatever staircase
of air it can find, people lift heavy tongues
needing new words, seeing the fearless army
of rain shattering again and again on pavement
but not having a name for that until the day
we drop, and the heart sends one final word.

THE LAST MAN WHO READ BOOKS

The last man who read books lived in them,
knew words could pull bricks apart,
find the push of fresh air. At his office
they step up to his counter and fill tight boxes
on forms with the weeds of their handwriting.
He sneered at them but knew books
could fix everything – maybe even him.

He knew even pain could be crafted.
Said *good morning all you insane people.*
Went home to think *I'll never get through this*,
and paused his lifetime of books dramatically
but didn't cry the words. Leaving the warm
embrace of a friend each day for the cold stare
on a streetcar, and trading the hush of paper
for the scrape of steel. Always, the pull and row

of people, the tug of war between those
who are kind and civil and those with hearts
that work like fists – clenched, unforgiving.
For every pair of warm eyes, two grey stones,
and for every shrub on a small bright hill, a cigar
stuck in the pale face of an old man –
the waiting room full, and listing like a galleon.

OLD MAN TRILOGY

1.

On the subway the old man next to me
talks at his wife, and she's so quiet
that I can only hear him, like listening
to a phone call, and the old guy begins
every sentence with I'll tell you something.
Hey old man, I'll tell you something:
two hundred and fifty million butterflies
just died in a freak cold snap,
probably caused by the way we fuck
with the earth. I'm trying to listen
as you ignore your wife, but can't hear
over the long, silent scream they gave,
background noise to most, like the subway.
I'm trying to read between the lines
of a paper to see what the push and pull,
all our millions of little actions, falling
together will do – I'd turn and explain
but you've got that phone call to make,
and I have mine. I've got my little rope
to pull and you've got yours, and honestly
I don't know how to let go of mine, either.

2.

A book doesn't know what impatience is,
and speaks as the old man flips forward,
then stops as he flips back again.
In the tunnel of a mall I shuffle forward
in line to buy an orange juice on my break,
watch the old man ignore weeping papers,

the fat belly of the security guard.
On some level my desire for a drink
is a small flame inside me, and we carry
a book of matches all day in the belly,
the whole human race moving great flames
into corners of the world. It worries me,
except there are books, dark bones of ink,
a shadow to think in before the blinding
white of the future. But nobody reads,
and I want to say show me, old man –
a book can take in ignorance like a whale,
simply moving and taking in plankton.
Show me, I think, as I walk past him,
back to the waiting elevators
that rise and fall like beating fists all day.

3.

Evidence arrived slowly: first the grey
that arrived silently in my hair, then
I noticed I was just as tall as my father,
but had always assumed he was taller.
Then I met someone with children,
and he was younger than me, not older.
And given that he was my height all along,
how did my father manage to be him,
to be intimidating, to seem like a father?
I heard the calm voice of an old man,
and saw it was my father, now retired.
I learned you don't wait for answers,
you spend your life, live and get them.
As quiet as noon, and as sudden
as someone putting a hand on my shoulder,
and my turning to see, I was a man.

KILLING INSECTS

When a roach is killed I utter a curse to accompany
the death but spiders (I have decided)
are more noble, and each time one is killed
a sad haiku that should have been written
goes quietly missing.

Is it true that when we kill an insect we don't
know if it was an ancestor back to watch us?
Some are either noble or stupid, holding
still while we close a tissue around it,
appearing to honour it, drape it in a cloak
before crushing it to a broken spot, legs torn off.

Is it true that when we die we feel
insect justice, every one we ever killed
crawling on our bodies while we offer
explanations: *Sorry, you surprised me in my kitchen*

at night but for what it's worth, I went back
to my lover in the dark and tried to find her
in the bed – her leg here and torso there, not
where I expected – crushed by the darkness.

OCTOBER

Standing at a train platform, I took some cold air
for myself, sunlight melting down my left side,
having spent the day with my sister and her almost
two-year-old son, watching him march over patterns
of crisp brown leaves I realized that history crouches

in all of us – that someday he'll be twenty
but I'll remember when he trusted the world so much
he ran his hand along the teeth of strange dogs
twice his size (eight years older than me,
my sister once taught me coins, lined up a quarter,
dime, nickel and one dark penny
And a nickel is worth five of those, before
I knew what men would do for money).

Then I moved to the bench at the station where sunlight
took the page I was turning and showed both sides
together, phrases surfacing on phrases, words
like piles of broken leaves – *feeling himself*
unsteady, through the empty rooms, the barometer
that his father used. Words in hidden seasons,

my sister's explanation for coins somewhere
at the base of my understanding of the word, digested.
The history I walk on as layers of scenes and words
and my nephew proudly home with a new one stored:
a dog is patient and bored, thick gums, and wet.

WORDS FOR A CRASHING COMPUTER

This heavy tool gives me nightmares:
I had internal bleeding, coughed blood
into snow at the side of causeway error 09.
My legs quiver and buckle, an unrecoverable
internal exception, my name wrapped in foil
before I chew it, invalid long filename entry.
Monitor, you're like an angry old woman,
I can see the noise hiding in your face.
Abort, Retry, Ignore, Fail? I made it
as far as a futile time capsule, a rotting barrel
with just a handful of red clay inside,
my limited hands waiting by the keyboard
like a couple of lost soft-shelled crabs
mistaking dull white bulbs for the sun,
and preening to show off thick wire hairs
before general failure, program terminated.

UNGATHERING

I rolled out my throat like a red carpet and
stood at the edge of it the way you might
stand at the edge of a pier – the music in this
bar is like invisible curtains, though they
don't prevent that woman from staring at me
while the man behind me is oblivious, I would hope,
to banging his chair against mine.
My voice is used and used to throw things out,
and you tell me things: why you decided
to become a Christian, how serious you are
about your new relationship, and I'm not sure
if I can call myself a Christian, but I sense
that we're like two generals on the same side
of a field, not quite making out what's out there,
writing short notes to each other, delayed
messages in handwriting that wavers slightly,
that betrays our knowledge of the ghosts
of frightened horses, guests who have gone out
the front door of our lives. There must be something
I can do, other than drop the thick, torn rug
of my voice on top of everything you say.

ALL NIGHT, WORLDS BLEND TOGETHER

Here in the jelly of night, we are hiding,
this apartment a box of light, our lantern
hanging off the street.
The string of lights out there
in the photo of this room
the window holds and shows me.

From a chair late at night, I ask letters
into place. Ink dark as night.
Somewhere a siren, faint emergency.

Sometimes the heartbeat of walking
above our ceiling – through the north wall
the giggle that tumbles in like a leak.

(We wake up some mornings to the orgasm
of the man above, the *oh oh* nails dropping
into air, a giant snapping his head back,
trying to inhale the world first thing).

The long tongue of a phone rings
and I can imagine it, *faint emergency.*
Suddenly a skin over the air in that room,
hear a chair jerk to life in response
as if at the end of a rope.

Hmmm, my love says, her arms thrown up
around her head – I wonder if someone
hears me creaking across floors for water
or if the noises nest like bats in her dreams.

An October leaf, the palm of a yellow hand
slapping the window startles me, as does
the flat crash of something dropped above.
The crack of high heels, that noise creeping up
my back belongs to old, grim schoolteachers.

See, I cannot keep the world out.

ONE

I sent you one of each possibility.

The letter didn't arrive from a stranger,
who staggered as if drunk, dropped it
without a thought. I saw a friend
on his way to you, watched him walk it
away, two sheets of folded white paper,
waving, white flag at the end of his arm.
The electronic mail arrived, sudden and
harmless as a garter snake, appearing
in the garden I picture behind your house.
I left my voice for you, bottled as it said

a few thoughts: *wondering how you are*
(my letter talked about people complaining
into the cold spaces we leave our voices,
I told you my suggestion, *if your voice
melts like new snow, add another layer).*
Waiting to hear from you, I finally imagine
the messages alive, sending a report
back from where the three had gathered.
There was no house – they kicked at dirt
where a campfire had burned, one turned

to another, said something was here.

MAN IN THE ENVELOPE OF DAY

He steps into the shower each morning
turns his face back and forth, lifts arms
as though in an ancient culture, worshipping
the heat of the sun. He stands on the subway
each morning – gently rocked, small thumbs
blackened with newsprint, feet stepping
on torn public faces. He brings his voice
to work, holds it between his arms tightly,
a drum – hums to the sound of his computer,
changes his signature from the dark insect it was
to a small, impotent tornado. He
doesn't remember when he last saw a sunrise,
gets home to wash his hands, watches them
fold together, dive after one another. At
dinner he lifts a knife, a tiny sword holding
his long reflection. Closes his eyes at night
mentally cutting around an image of himself
only to discard it, hold up the flimsy outline
saying *none of this will happen now.*

AT THE DEVIL'S PUNCHBOWL

The office began to own me, paid me to fuss.
The pen behind my ear a little missile,
brought out for my latest stapler metaphor.
Dreamed of the day I snapped, alone on the streetcar,
agreed to marry someone's choice of lawyer.
But the Devil's Punchbowl was all about perspective:
this, by the way, is what it's like to stand
a hundred feet underground thanks to the giant
curving cup of earth removed. On the surface,
where the water charged off to fall halfway
past brown layers of earth to burst, patiently
again and again on the spot where the rock
jutted out, a lone man appeared like an apparition,
considered suicide but maybe looked down,
decided he couldn't scar the lives below.
If I could make a sound at once for everything
that I don't know the answer might lie there,
in the mud and endless patience of slow erosion.
Part of the answer was to go to the bottom first,
watch children scrabble around like fleas and then
climb out to the top to look down, simply stand
where another incomplete man stood, knowing
we could get down, and we could get out as well.

THE BURNING ENGLISH CANADIAN KNOWS SOMETHING IS MISSING FROM HIS LIFE

The flames on him are transparent, only he
sees them, and they move thickly with him,
as slow and hidden as the sure dance of seaweed.
He always has seconds left, leans on the angle
of a street corner, sees pigeons take off
above a man in the shape of a broken crown
and knows it's a sign, learns we're all a mixture
of pavement and stars, and he must drive east
for hours, burning hands on the wheel inside
the bright yellow paint of summer heat.
In Montréal he slows alongside a woman
on a bike eating ice cream, just two fistfuls of sunlight
for a helmet, hair dyed the colour
of a hillside audience of bluebells lectured by air.
An old man smiles, crow perched on a red
motorbike, young man on a green bike opposite.

The burning man walks, tries not to stagger,
proposes to a gracefully swimming smile,
is gently rebuffed, moves on to Québec City
to walk the plains of Abraham, imagines muskets.
He visits Montmorency Falls: one smooth shoulder,
two long unfolding white arms, and below
the slow breathing of pooled logs undulating.
The granite Église St-Jean at Île d'Orléans
looks like a ship sitting on the river, and flowers
on a cemetery plot take the shape of an anchor.
Inside, the porcelain angel nods at each coin,
as he lights two candles for two struggling fathers.
On a patio he's thinking there must be answers

simpler than history when a waitress slops beer
on his foot – *Merde*, she says but he only smiles,
having heard the hiss that rose up as a flame went out.

MY HEART IN A CHEAP BROWN SUIT

My heart stopped believing we're all in this
together and left for America: I got a photo
of it, smiling with Las Vegas hookers.
Postcards said look, I pulled the cord
and started up thirty times over thirty cups
of coffee but none of it was anything.
It complained there were only some good days,
when instead of getting on the subway car
and finding everyone staring, half asleep clutching
papers, we met something different, an old cowboy
head to toe in yellow, eyes closed
concentrating on his six feet of brightness.

It watched a man sit cross-legged near the edge
of the platform, serious and tapping his hands,
then he stood up as the train arrived,
took one step and stopped, and it knew
he was practicing, but didn't say anything to him
out of some notion that it's his business.
Reading the postcards, I sense what was near it,
whistle of workers and clatter of ladders as
it sat in a stairwell, businessman in a black suit
on the bus next to it, body plump as a question
mark, sharp smell from his package of peanuts.
In the loopy handwriting, the jerking of the bus.

TO NITE ONLY

All chalk and dust, the sign outside the bar
reminds me every day TO NITE ONLY
and not another word.

Days I pass it, thick blue padlocked doors,
and sunlight finds the word a finger wrote: SHIT.
Arrive at work to hook the dark insect
of a phone over my ear,
let strangers sculpt the only sounds.

Nights I pass it, a bar the size of a bedroom,
watch a businessman outside
lean on the wall like a friend and vomit
while other men laugh.
So I wander out, step quickly around

the old lady, her lion of white hair and cane
that goes a thousand miles into the earth but
to nite only, for all I know, is all I have.

WAITING FOR A POEM

You will have to excuse the stick figure,
the letter *I* popping up in this forest
of letters, the poet waiting,
like an eccentric butterfly catcher, crouched
with a net outside the clearing.
His hand rests on his thigh and he remembers
things, one night when his tongue
met the small cherry of a nipple and
oh, the noise. There is a flash
of colour that surfaces from the undergrowth
and darts through the clearing, but the poet
stays still, holding his net
because that was not anything, really.
He thinks of the fat man he saw, some unknown
force pulling him one step after another,
down the subway platform in his pink socks,
but still he does not move to lift his hand.
I don't know who he is, the poet, but I need him,
am waiting for him. I am a man
of few words because I wait for better ones.

HILLS OF INSTANTS

Washing dishes I notice
two quiet knives in a bowl,
insist that it is evening: ten to nine.

What I find falling off lips,
passing down the air in front of me
is that we are mostly nothing –
water, space between atoms.

And how much of our lives
are these small white bricks:
my reaching out absently to
poke knives into a new position.

Striking moments flashing out
the way a lighthouse is on
top of so much nothing.

THE MORNING AFTER A COLLEAGUE DIES IN A MOTORCYCLE ACCIDENT

You'll be sitting at your desk at work when
you open an email saying he deid, was killd –
written by someone clearly upset, and you
remember his easy laugh, black leather jacket,
and know his thick hands growing fish cold
will never hold his two daughters again.
And the way that you found out, so technical,
somehow adds to it – was somehow wrong,
an email sneaking in that way, like cancer.
You trained with him for just four full weeks
before being shipped to different offices,
and even you remember him, are moved.

He was a man who rose above the bite
of paperwork, his laughter rolled over desks,
could not be pinned to boards, his smile
broke his bald round head in two with white.
You're expected to work, your mind holds back.
And you hesitate before pressing the last button.
To complete the call somehow allows the world
to carry on, a connection springing up
on some line where sparrows currently rest.
The office hums around you, no one here
can discuss it. You wait a few more seconds,
press the button, the call goes through.

THE SOUND OF HISTORY

People thundering up wooden steps (find
the sound, you know it) is the sound of history,
suddenly becomes the same thing people
heard decades ago, when this house
was in a clearing with forest around,
no cold talk overhead between skyscrapers,
and that street was the long, winding driveway.
Here we forget history was brutal, just
in different ways, here everything meets:
staff in nineteenth-century clothing tap
away on computers while silently outside
a ladybug moves backwards on the plaque,
from m to o in *prominent,* not knowing to care.

BURIED DEEP AMONG THE LIVING

I.

Stayed home today and wrote and watched TV
and read and washed dishes and watched people
walk the street and ran my mind over it
to mark the day with a tiny flag: worthy.
Like most days I missed the slow announcement
of dawn, the light winning silent battles for corners.
It seems to me our lives are an announcement
that goes on so long few people listen.
so I went outside, just to be counted
among those walking the earth, even if only
to cross the street for a newspaper and chocolate.

II.

Came back for the slow announcement of night,
The darkness winning now. It seems warmer.
Just yesterday the window had icicles like bars.
And a memory reappeared of a very old woman
taking her napkin, folding it over and neatly
from years of habit. It hardly mattered – it was
just a paper napkin about to be thrown out,
as she already had been, dropped
in the human parking lot of an old folks home.
But folding the napkin was what she did.
It meant something to her, so I just sat and watched.

DESIRING A FRIEND

Whatever has been pressed
into the shape of your hands
catches my attention,

the small dance of bringing
your cigarette to life. Pointed elsewhere,
everyone else missed that.

And somewhere now, a man
who may be lucky enough
one day to place kisses
on the small train of your spine,
opens a door, steps outside.

But your hands while I listen,
your hands while you explain
anything will move like birds,
separate but loyal to you.
There is a photograph of you
with your arm around me, your
hand finding a space to rest
on my shoulder.

Saying goodbye, I spun you around
and your laughter fell in my ear,
and fell asleep there.

This is what I have, and so
this is what I will have to want,
that laughter, or your hands
across from me now,

my thoughts moving over you
around walls, down streets
like a broken army looking
for the heart of the city
it turns constantly away from,
then back.

WINTER

Winter paints the landscape white as bone
then white again, wanting clarity,
wanting it all to emerge one thing at a time.
Bare trees just manage to hold the quiet earth down.

Inside, we are so deeply intertwined,
I almost moved to kiss my own hand.

While outside, faces on posters angrily
defaced for trying to sell useless things,
shiver, beam, and shiver through the night.

POSTCARDS

1.

A part of me is jealous of books, and wishes
to be over, sealed like the neat lines of a biography,
the black and white photo of me looking back
over my shoulder. This is a poem for you.
Someday you'll read this, say he got his wish.

2.

Trying to get things from my mind, a ball from a dog,
wanting to relax and read. I wonder if sleep
or activity will wash the tired like paint from my eyes.
When my arm rests near my chest I feel the lungs
gently rise and fall and somehow I think of a child
on a swing in a park sailing back and forth.

3.

A part of me wants to remember to feel the air
around me, run fingertips over bark
and brick and the skin of another.
A part of me is pacing, asks why we rush
everywhere, are shaped inside to collect anger,
simply expect food to be in stores, teach children
someone may push them in front of the subway train.

4.

I don't really want my death, to be replaced
with books but I wish for a life that steps out

of balance just often enough
to know that it's fine all the time. And someday,
wherever I am after death, or even if I
am gone, only half-hidden in the darkness
of ink, this is what I'd wish for you.

THE WAY THE AFTERLIFE BEGINS

The cat, as something familiar, moves up the path
towards you while you puzzle it out – a cat
that should be dead, and up the hill the house
where people lift their arms in greeting from
the yard and you can almost tell who.
The house surrounded by trees and all you need.
Resting arrowhead of cat with folded legs,
points the way, you remember how you got there:
trees marched endlessly by the side of the road,
the landscape changed too slowly for you to notice.
You remember her eyes, in your life you'd looked
into them and knew they'd melt – two pools of snow
that couldn't last, no matter how much they should.

You learn things about your life already lived:
that the impassive kindergarten teacher you hated
for spanking you was filled with regret,
dreamed of vengeful children, hurled lunchboxes,
her eyes mistaken for grapes by a starved child,
insatiable desires to touch hot stoves,
and the hand she hit with amputated in an accident.
You learn that the man you so kindly gave directions
doubled back and was killed by a car,
that books remember fingertips like faces.
That you turned off the alarm, and half asleep
held the clock against your chest, as though a heart
or to encourage the one you had – keep on going.

MARQUIS
MEMBER OF SCABRINI GROUP
Québec, Canada
2007